Disney
AT THE PIANO

ISBN 0-634-00416-6

Walt Disney Music Company
Wonderland Music Company, Inc.

DISTRIBUTED BY

HAL•LEONARD®
CORPORATION
7777 W. BLUEMOUND RD. P.O. BOX 13819 MILWAUKEE, WI 53213

Visit Hal Leonard Online at
www.halleonard.com

Disney
AT THE PIANO

The Bare Necessities

from Walt Disney's THE JUNGLE BOOK

Words and Music by
TERRY GILKYSON

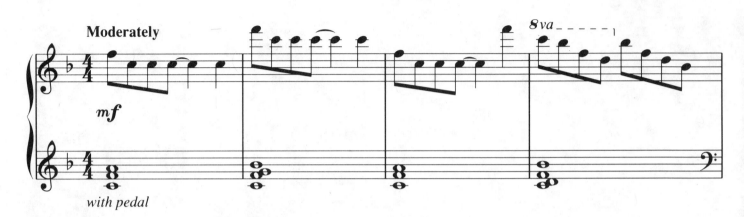

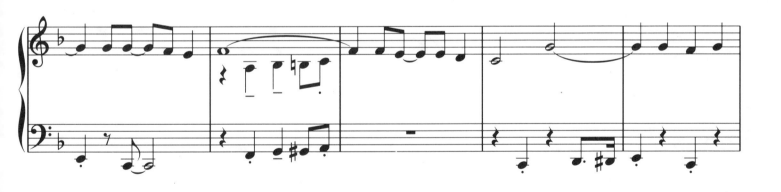

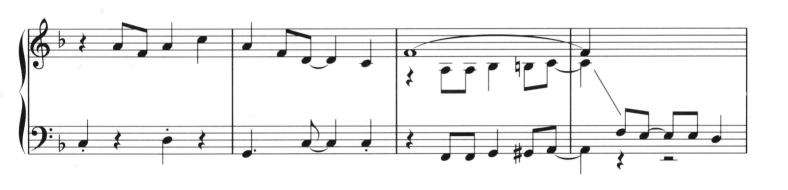

Colors of the Wind
from Walt Disney's POCAHONTAS

Music by ALAN MENKEN
Lyrics by STEPHEN SCHWARTZ

Moderately, expressively

Beauty and the Beast
from Walt Disney's BEAUTY AND THE BEAST

Lyrics by HOWARD ASHMAN
Music by ALAN MENKEN

Candle on the Water

from Walt Disney's PETE'S DRAGON

Words and Music by AL KASHA
and JOEL HIRSCHHORN

hold pedal to end

Circle of Life
from Walt Disney Pictures' THE LION KING

Music by ELTON JOHN
Lyrics by TIM RICE

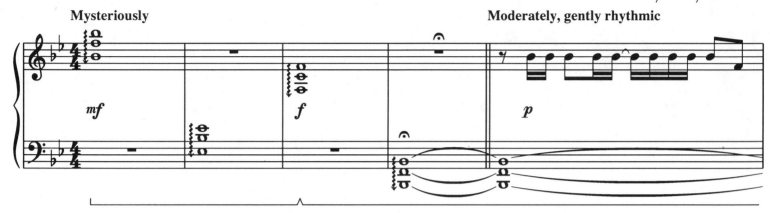

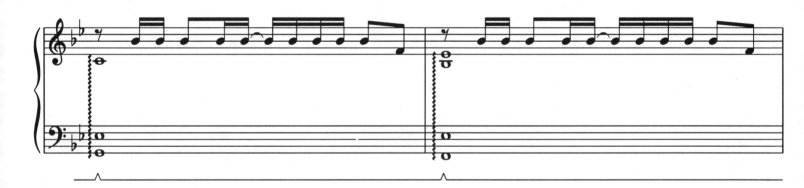

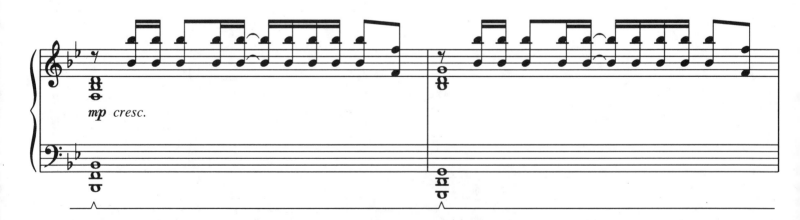

cresc

f

(With pedal)

Top two notes

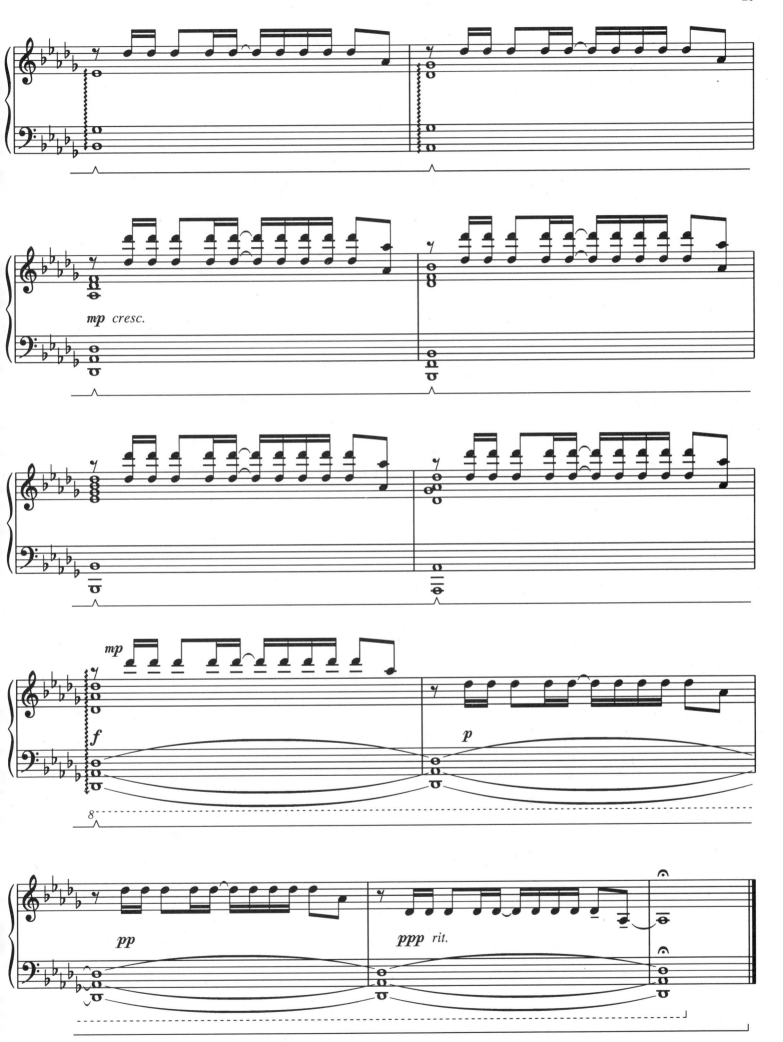

A Dream Is a Wish Your Heart Makes

from Walt Disney's CINDERELLA

Words and Music by MACK DAVID,
AL HOFFMAN and JERRY LIVINGSTON

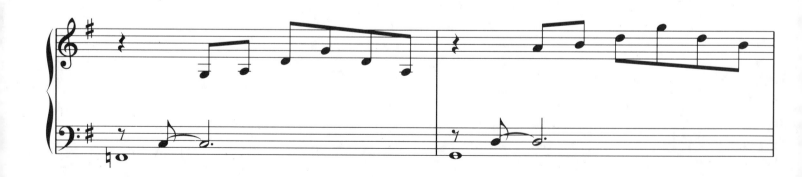

Tenderly

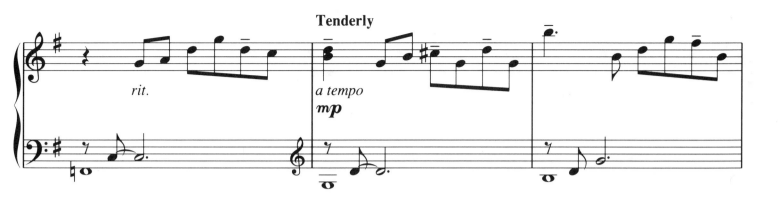

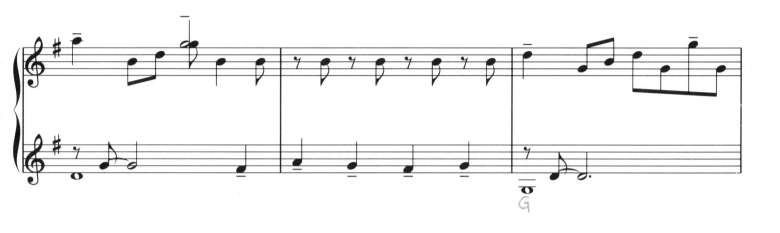

Friend Like Me

from Walt Disney's ALADDIN

Lyrics by HOWARD ASHMAN
Music by ALAN MENKEN

8va bassa

It's a Small World

from Disneyland and Walt Disney World's IT'S A SMALL WORLD

Words and Music by ROBERT M. SHERMAN
and ROBERT B. SHERMAN

Playful Waltz

God Help the Outcasts

from Walt Disney's THE HUNCHBACK OF NOTRE DAME

Music by ALAN MENKEN
Lyrics by STEPHEN SCHWARTZ

Mickey Mouse March

from Walt Disney's THE MICKEY MOUSE CLUB

Words and Music by
JIMMIE DODD

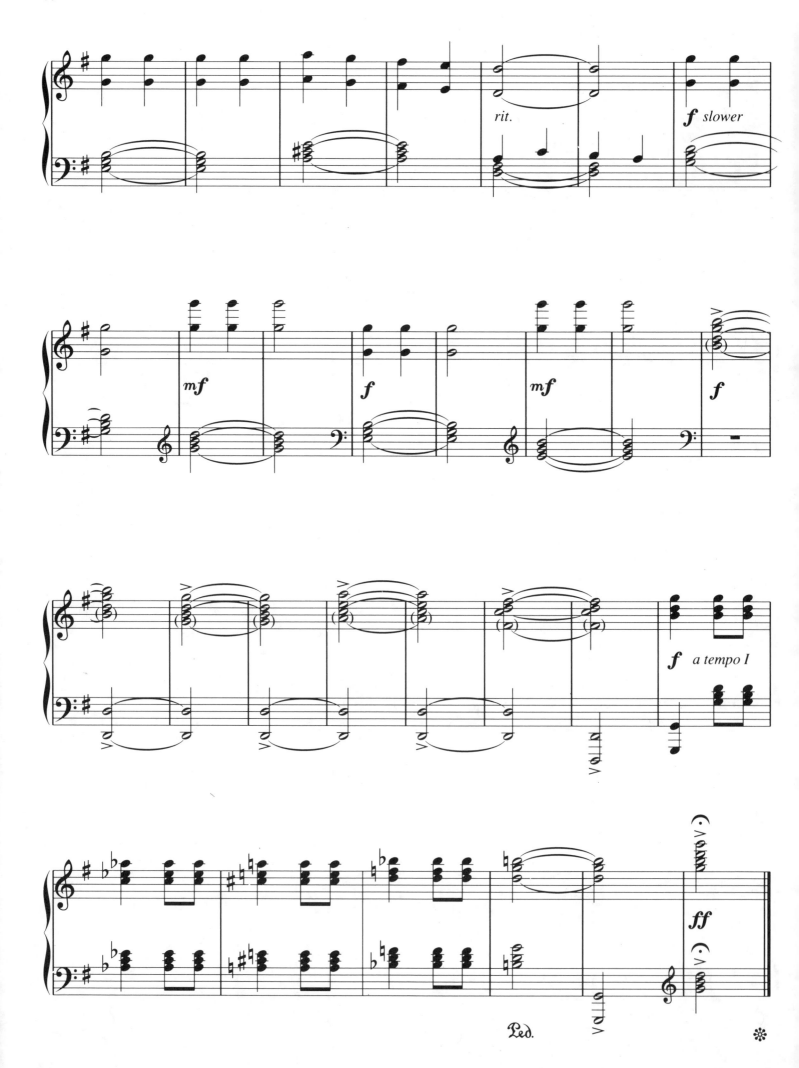

Once Upon a Dream

from Walt Disney's SLEEPING BEAUTY

Words and Music by SAMMY FAIN
and JACK LAWRENCE
Adapted from a Theme by TCHAIKOVSKY

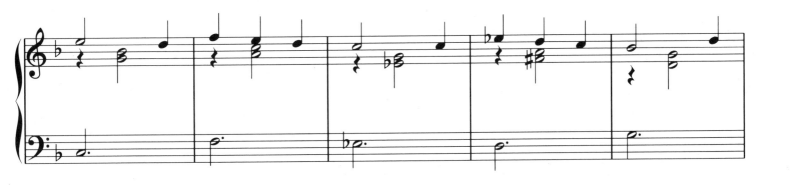

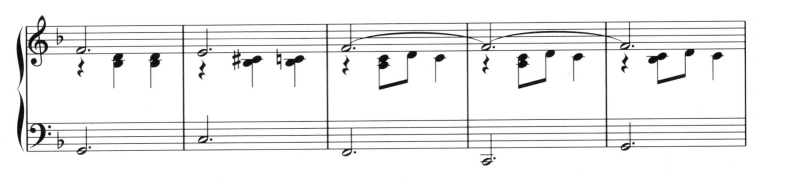

The Time of Your Life

from Walt Disney's A BUG'S LIFE

Words and Music by
RANDY NEWMAN

Under the Sea
from Walt Disney's THE LITTLE MERMAID

Lyrics by HOWARD ASHMAN
Music by ALAN MENKEN

Medium Calypso

Where Do I Go from Here

from Walt Disney's POCAHONTAS II: JOURNEY TO A NEW WORLD

Music by LARRY GROSSMAN
Words by MARTY PANZER